MILTON'S BIG IDEA

MILTON'S BIG IDEA

A Color Me Story
About judging, bullying and
courage!

WRITTEN BY CAROL MARIE FIGONI
ILLUSTRATED BY KATIELYNN REMILLARD

IGLOOS

Igloos are no longer a common type of housing. Actually, it is hard to even find one in the Artic regions these days.

Historically, Inuit across the Arctic lived in igloos before the introduction of modern, European–style homes. These remarkable structures, ingeniously designed by indigenous peoples of the polar regions, have not only provided shelter in extreme cold but also hold cultural and historical significance. Igloos also retain practical value: some hunters and those seeking emergency shelter still use them.

BOOK DEDICATION

This book is dedictated to everyone who has ever been bullied.

We each have our own unique gifts that make us special. That is what makes the world so interesting! It's hard to realize this when you are young and stand out from the crowd in an awkward or uncomfortable way.

As people mature, they often strive to be more unique and even unusual. Many artists, musicians, and inventors are good examples of this. They realize that being different can be a good thing. It is something to embrace and be proud of.

If you look different, feel different, think, or speak differently, try to remember that you are a unique special shining star in this vast universe. Those who are bullying you probably know that deep down inside. What sets you apart is amazing and most likely will eventually become your greatest asset in one way or another!

In the small village of
Iceberg, Alaska lived
a man by the name
of Milton Miller.

He and his family lived
in a beautiful igloo on
Snowy Hill Road.

There were many families who lived in beautiful igloos on Snowy Hill Road.

SNOWY HILL
RD.

One day Milton had a
brilliant idea!
He had just thought of
a new way to make their
igloo warmer during the
cold winter months ahead.

Milton made a trip to
Pete's Hardware
to buy some
black spray paint.

PETE'S HARDWARE

Early the next morning
Milton got to work.
He spray painted his
entire igloo black!

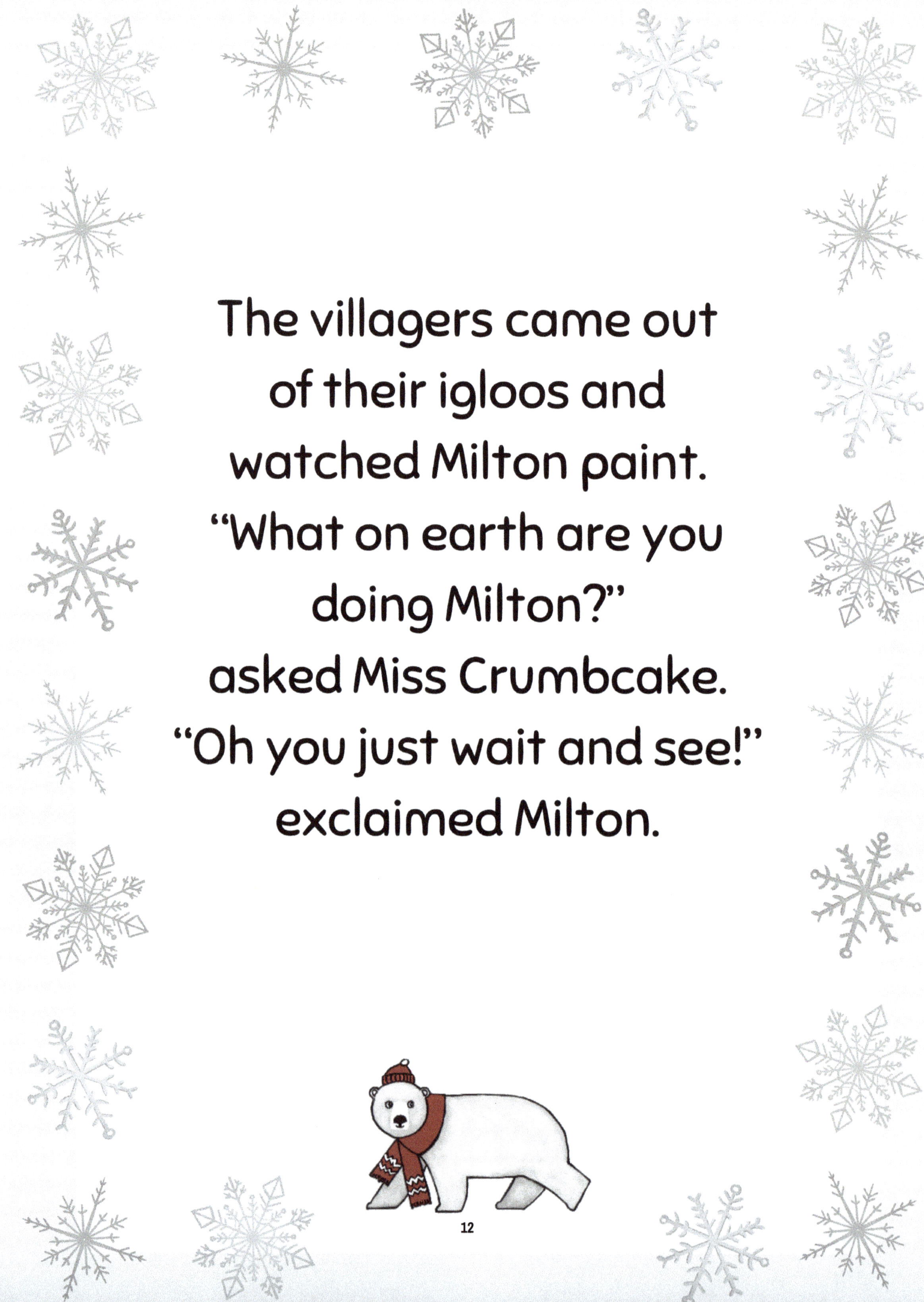

The villagers came out
of their igloos and
watched Milton paint.
"What on earth are you
doing Milton?"
asked Miss Crumbcake.
"Oh you just wait and see!"
exclaimed Milton.

The next day Milton and
his family felt extra warm
and cozy inside their igloo!
"My idea worked!"
exclaimed Milton.
"What idea?"
asked his son.

Milton explained that
since darker colors
absorb more sunlight
than lighter colors,
their igloo was warmer
now because it was black.

ABSORBS
REFLECTS

Milton bragged to
everyone in the village
about his brilliant idea
and Pete's Hardware was
sold out of black paint
by the end of the day.

SUPPLIES
BLACK PAINT
SOLD OUT

The next day every igloo
on Snowy Hill Road
was painted black.
All except for one.

SNOWY HILL
RD.

Miss Crumbcake refused
to paint her igloo black.
"It's a bad idea,"
she said.

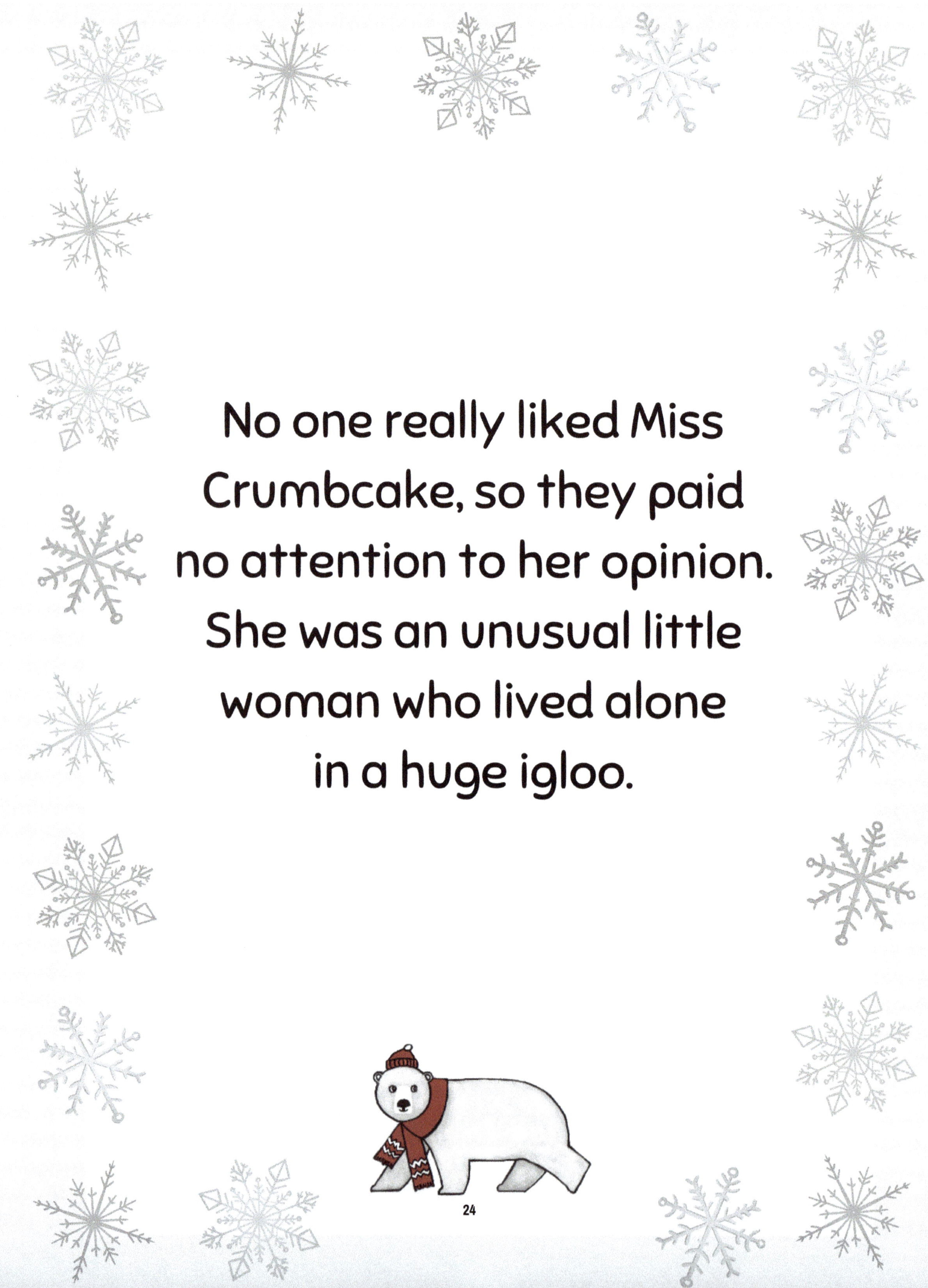

No one really liked Miss
Crumbcake, so they paid
no attention to her opinion.
She was an unusual little
woman who lived alone
in a huge igloo.

25

For a few days everyone
on Snowy Hill Road
was thrilled with their
extra warm homes.
Milton was the village hero!

The sun shined down on the black igloos and made them extra toasty warm inside.

Then something terrible
started to happen.
The igloos were getting
smaller and the floors
were getting wet.
Milton could hardly fit
through his front door.

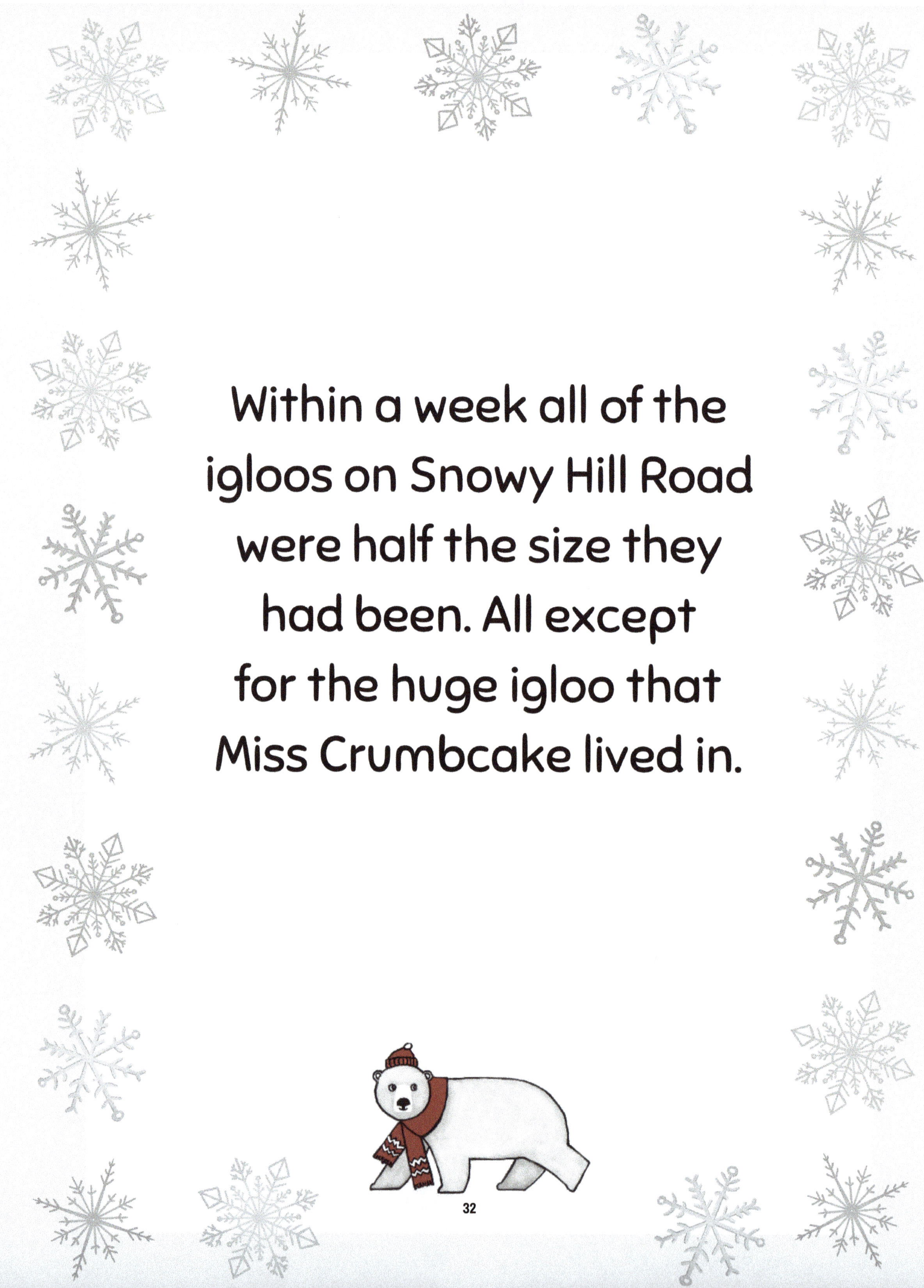

Within a week all of the igloos on Snowy Hill Road were half the size they had been. All except for the huge igloo that Miss Crumbcake lived in.

SNOWY HILL
RD.
33

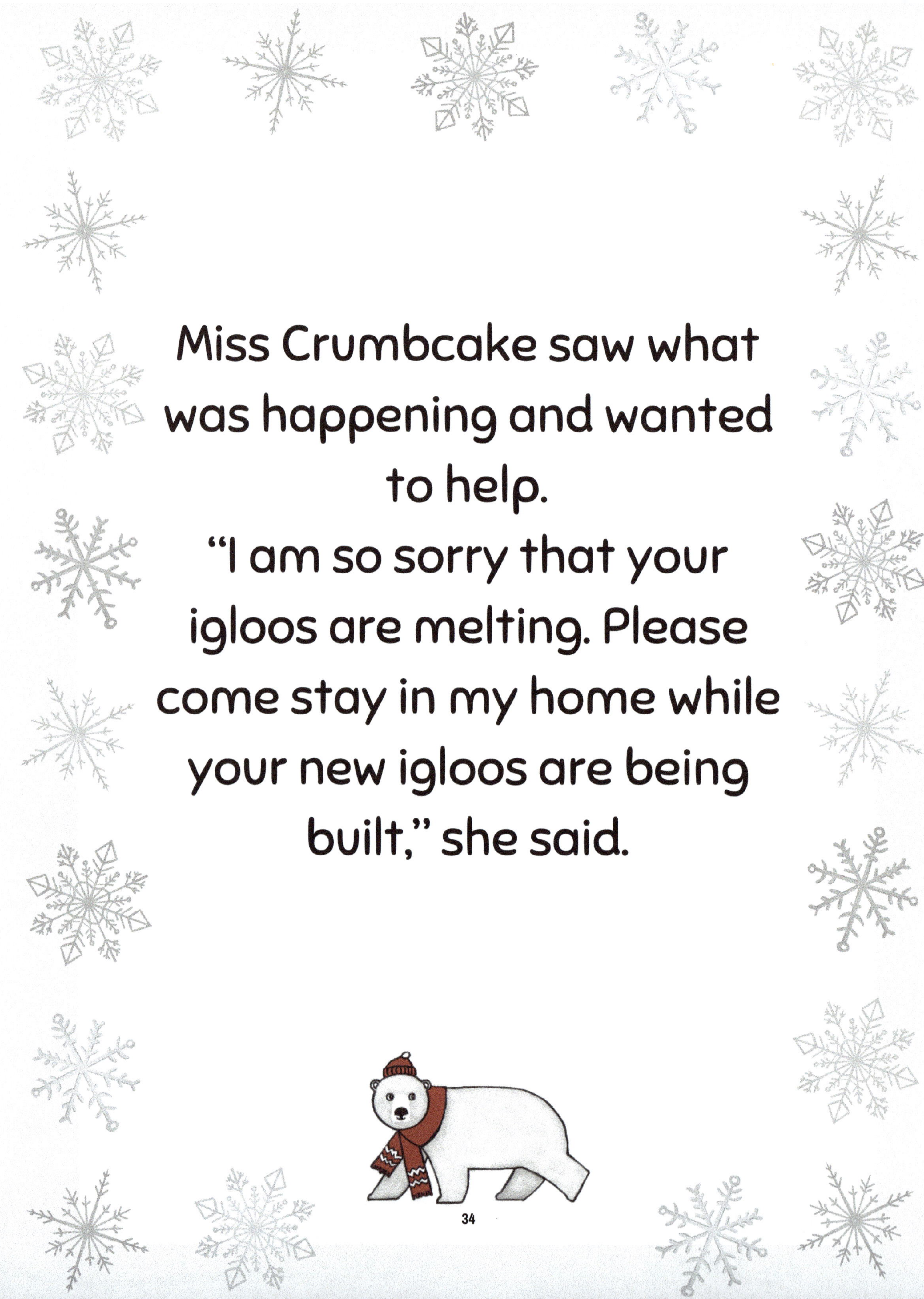

Miss Crumbcake saw what was happening and wanted to help.
"I am so sorry that your igloos are melting. Please come stay in my home while your new igloos are being built," she said.

The next day everyone
got to work building their
new igloos. Some people
bullied Milton, because
his idea had failed.
Milton felt sad.
Miss Crumbcake felt bad
for Milton. She knew what it
felt like to be bullied.

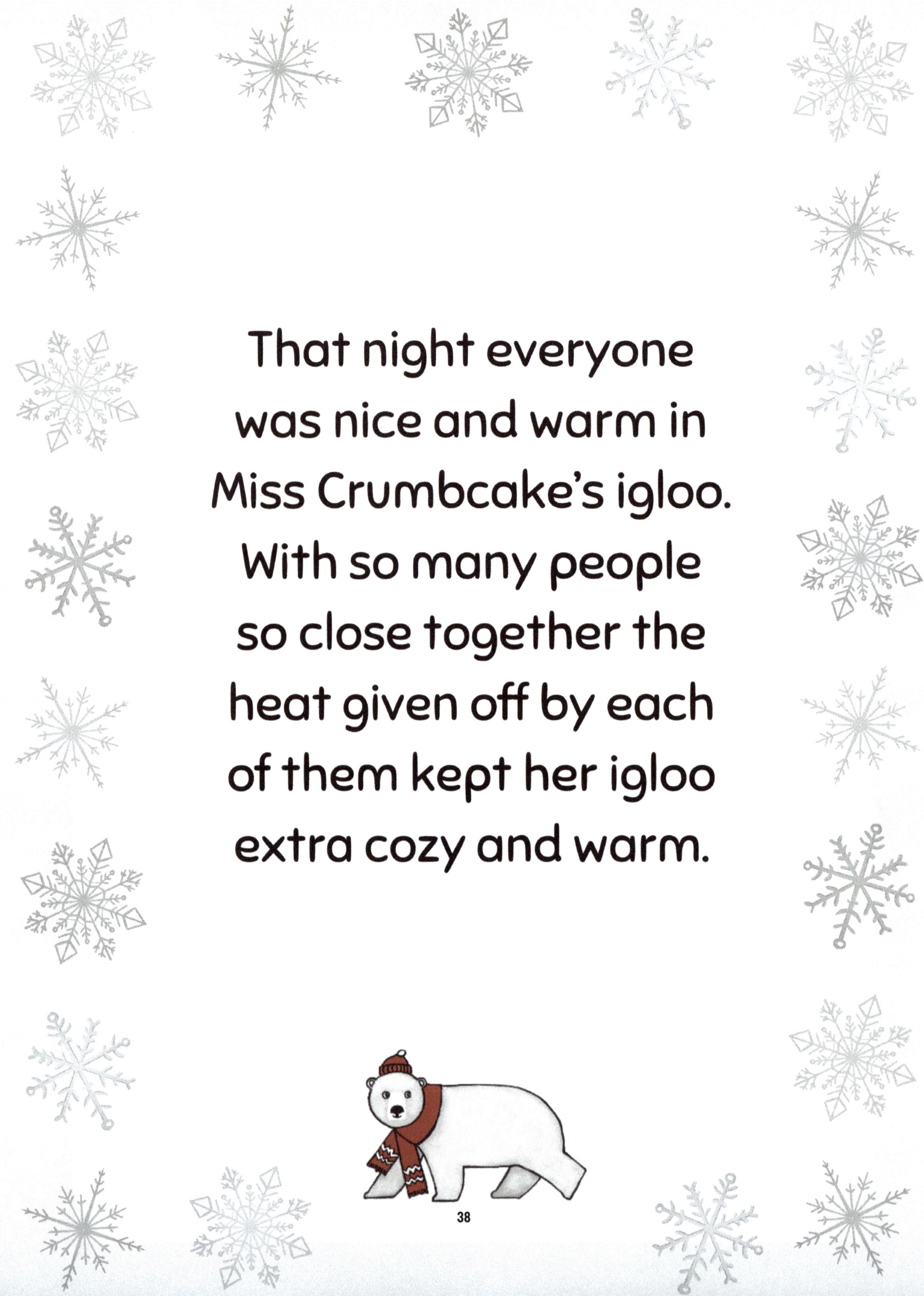

That night everyone
was nice and warm in
Miss Crumbcake's igloo.
With so many people
so close together the
heat given off by each
of them kept her igloo
extra cozy and warm.

This gave Milton another
idea!
"Maybe we should build our
new igloos a little smaller?"
he shyly suggested.
"Yes! That is a brilliant idea!"
exclaimed Miss Crumbcake.

WARM

After much thought and discussion, it was decided that the new igloos would be built smaller. This way the heat from their bodies would have less space to warm up and they would stay warmer during the cold winter months ahead.

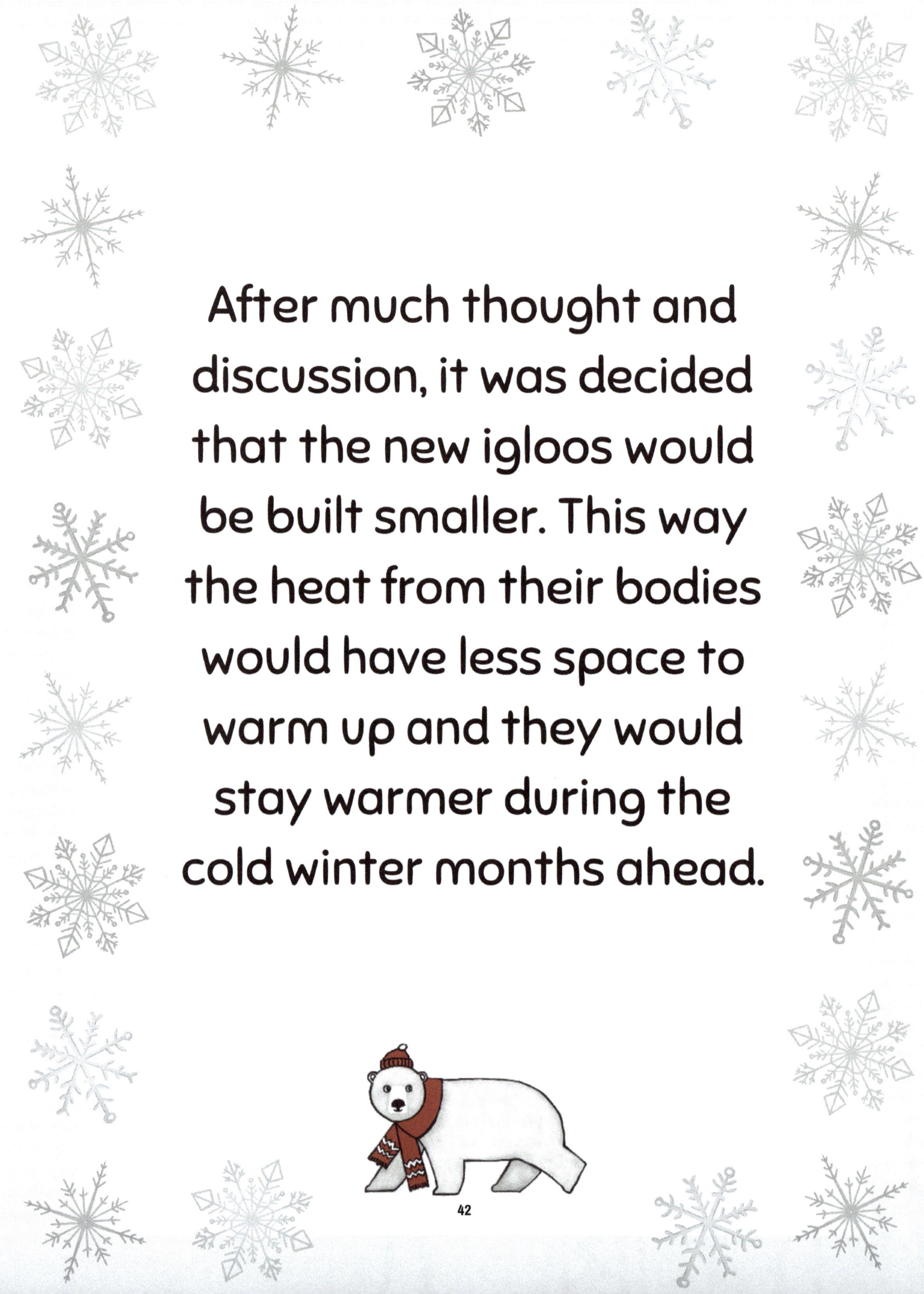

Miss Crumbcake even
decided to have a smaller
igloo built for herself.
Milton was once again
the village hero and
Miss Crumbcake had a
village full of new friends!

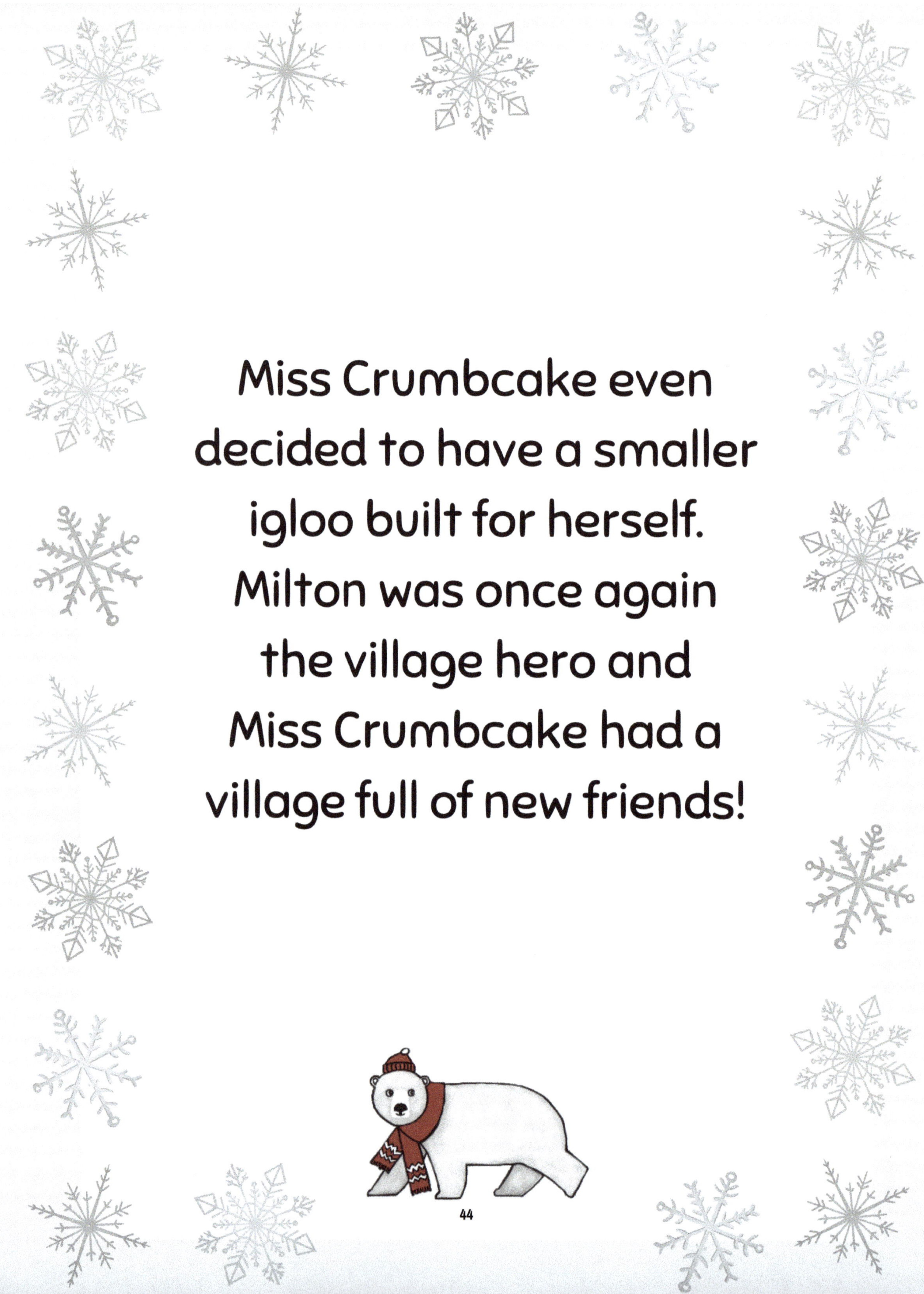

<u>LESSONS IN THIS BOOK TO DISCUSS:</u>

JUDGING PEOPLE BY HOW THEY LOOK ISN'T FAIR

1. Why do you think no one liked Miss Crumbcake?
2. Was it because she looked unusual?
3. Is that fair?
4. Have you ever not liked someone because they looked different than most people?
5. What did everyone learn about Miss Crumbcake once they got to know her better?
6. Do you know the saying, "Don't judge a book by its cover?"
7. What exactly do you think that means?

SUPPORT INVENTORS AND ACCEPT THAT IT IS OKAY TO FAIL

1. Who was the inventor in this story?
2. Did you think his first idea was a good idea?
3. Why do you think Milton was shy about suggesting his second idea?
4. Have you ever been shy about suggesting one of your ideas? Why?
5. How many times do you think inventors fail before they have an idea that is a great success?
6. Are you glad inventors don't give up, even when their ideas don't always work out?

DON'T BE AFRAID TO STAND ALONE FOR WHAT YOU BELIEVE

1. Do you know what the saying "Black Sheep" means?
2. Who was the Black Sheep in this story?
3. Do you admire Miss Crumbcake for not following the crowd?
4. Do you admire Milton for not giving up on his creative new ideas?
5. Who do you think was bullied in this story?
6. What is bullying?
7. Is putting people down or ignoring them a type of bullying?
8. What are other types of bullying?
9. Why do you think some people bully others?

TEST OUT NEW IDEAS BEFORE JUMPING IN TOO FAST

1. What should the villagers have done before they copied Milton's first idea?
2. Did they do that with his second idea?
3. Have you ever jumped into something too fast and had it not work out?

BONUS QUESTION!

1. What color do you think would be best to wear on a hot summer day?

"The world would be a very boring place
if everyone was alike!"
~My Mom

Nicholas

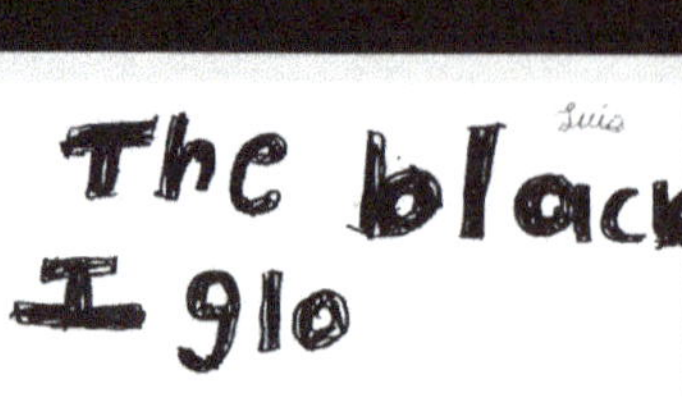

The black
I glo

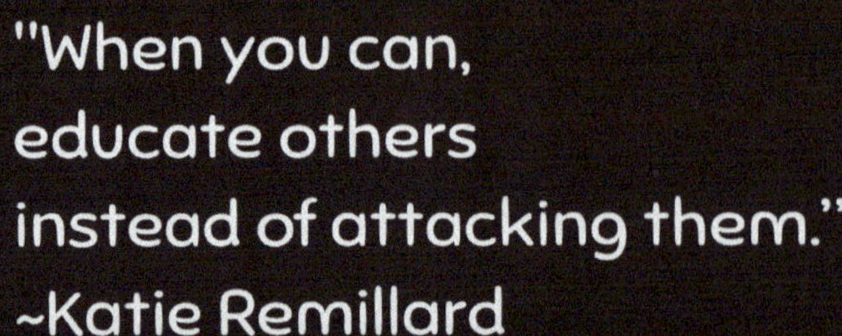

"When you can,
educate others
instead of attacking them."
~Katie Remillard

The thing about art is that there are no mistakes and the most valuable pieces are unique and sometimes a little weird... just like us!"
~ Dia Shay Figoni

Find something you
have in common
and you will find a friend.
~ Carol Marie Figoni

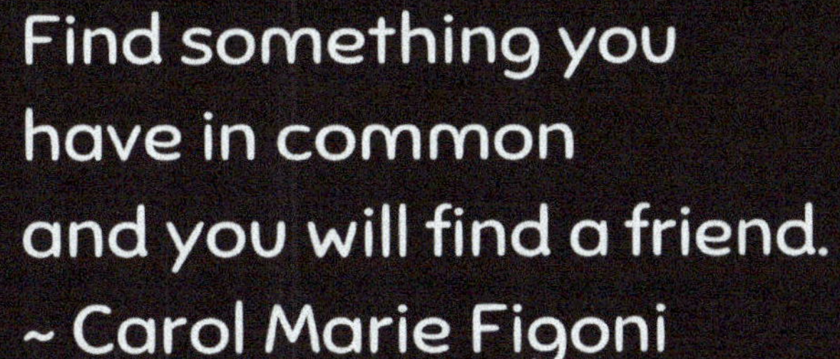

Be A Buddy, Not A Bully!

HOW WOULD YOU COLOR THE FRONT COVER?

52

MILTON'S BIG IDEA

Meet the Author

CAROL MARIE FIGONI

This is Book #1 of "Little Life Lessons" by Carol Marie Figoni. When Carol's children were young, she started writing little stories with life lessons in them. Now that her children are grown, she is publishing these stories for everyone to enjoy!

Carol was born and raised in California. Her childhood was challenging due to severe speech problems and serious issues with her feet. She learned at a young age what it felt like to be bullied. This gave her compassion for people from all walks of life.

Her mother is a talented artist and her father was a brilliant engineer. Carol graduated from The Fashion Institute of Designing and Merchandising and worked as a fashion designer for many years. She has always had a desire to create, invent and try new things!

Meet the illustrator

KATIELYNN REMILLARD

Katielynn Remillard drew all of the adorable illustrations for Milton's Big Idea!

She is a twenty one year old talented artist who has always had a drive and passion for art. She graduated early from high school at age sixteen, because of bullying and found that art really helped her through the hard times.

She has been drawing for over fifteen years and loves every opportunity that has come her way. She has done everything from simple line drawings to sculptures. Her biggest inspiration in life is her family and the support they have always given her.

FACEBOOK ♡ MILTONSBIGIDEA
INSTAGRAM @MILTONSBIGIDEA